JOEL HORWOOD

Joel is an associate artist of the ⸻Hammersmith Theatre, whose work has been performed throughout the UK. Recent credits include *The Little Mermaid* (Bristol Old Vic Theatre), *The Planet and Stuff* (Polka Theatre), *I Heart Peterborough* (Eastern Angles/Soho Theatre), *A Stab in the Dark* and *A Series of Increasingly Impossible Acts* (Lyric Hammersmith, Secret Theatre). Other credits include *The Count of Monte Cristo* (West Yorkshire Playhouse), *I Caught Crabs in Walberswick* (Eastern Angels at the Pleasance/UK tour/Bush), *Food* (Traverse Theatre) which received a Fringe First Award, and *Mikey the Pikey* (Pleasance/UK tour).

Other Plays for Young People to Perform from Nick Hern Books

Original Plays

100
Christopher Heimann,
Neil Monaghan, Diene Petterle

BLOOD AND ICE
Liz Lochhead

BOYS
Ella Hickson

BUNNY
Jack Thorne

BURYING YOUR BROTHER IN THE
PAVEMENT
Jack Thorne

CHRISTMAS IS MILES AWAY
Chloë Moss

COCKROACH
Sam Holcroft

THE DOMINO EFFECT
AND OTHER PLAYS
Fin Kennedy

DISCO PIGS
Enda Walsh

EIGHT
Ella Hickson

GIRLS LIKE THAT
Evan Placey

HOW TO DISAPPEAR COMPLETELY
AND NEVER BE FOUND
Fin Kennedy

I CAUGHT CRABS IN
WALBERSWICK
Joel Horwood

KINDERTRANSPORT
Diane Samuels

MOGADISHU
Vivienne Franzmann

MOTH
Declan Greene

THE MYSTAE
Nick Whitby

OVERSPILL
Ali Taylor

PRONOUN
Evan Placey

SAME
Deborah Bruce

THERE IS A WAR
Tom Basden

THE URBAN GIRL'S GUIDE TO
CAMPING AND OTHER PLAYS
Fin Kennedy

THE WARDROBE
Sam Holcroft

Adaptations

ANIMAL FARM
Ian Wooldridge
Adapted from George Orwell

ARABIAN NIGHTS
Dominic Cooke

BEAUTY AND THE BEAST
Laurence Boswell

CORAM BOY
Helen Edmundson
Adapted from Jamila Gavin

DAVID COPPERFIELD
Alastair Cording
Adapted from Charles Dickens

GREAT EXPECTATIONS
Nick Ormerod and Declan Donnellan
Adapted from Charles Dickens

HIS DARK MATERIALS
Nicholas Wright
Adapted from Philip Pullman

THE JUNGLE BOOK
Stuart Paterson
Adapted from Rudyard Kipling

KENSUKE'S KINGDOM
Stuart Paterson
Adapted from Michael Morpurgo

KES
Lawrence Till
Adapted from Barry Hines

THE LOTTIE PROJECT
Vicky Ireland
Adapted from Jacqueline Wilson

MIDNIGHT
Vicky Ireland
Adapted from Jacqueline Wilson

NOUGHTS & CROSSES
Dominic Cooke
Adapted from Malorie Blackman

THE RAILWAY CHILDREN
Mike Kenny
Adapted from E. Nesbit

SWALLOWS AND AMAZONS
Helen Edmundson and Neil Hannon
Adapted from Arthur Ransome

TO SIR, WITH LOVE
Ayub Khan-Din
Adapted from E.R Braithwaite

TREASURE ISLAND
Stuart Paterson
Adapted from Robert Louis Stevenson

WENDY & PETER PAN
Ella Hickson
Adapted from J.M. Barrie

THE WOLVES OF WILLOUGHBY
CHASE
Russ Tunney
Adapted from Joan Aiken

Joel Horwood

THIS CHANGES EVERYTHING

NICK HERN BOOKS
www.nickhernbooks.co.uk

TONIC THEATRE
www.tonictheatre.co.uk

A Nick Hern Book

This Changes Everything first published as a paperback original in Great Britain in 2015 by Nick Hern Books Limited, The Glasshouse, 49a Goldhawk Road, London W12 8QP, in association with Tonic Theatre

This Changes Everything copyright © 2015 Joel Horwood

Joel Horwood has asserted his right to be identified as the author of this work

Cover image by Kathy Barber, Bullet Creative, www.bulletcreative.com

Designed and typeset by Nick Hern Books, London
Printed and bound in Great Britain by Mimeo Ltd, Huntingdon, Cambridgeshire PE29 6XX

A CIP catalogue record for this book is available from the British Library

ISBN   978 1 84842 500 2

Woodland
CARBON
www.woodlandcarbon.co.uk
NICK HERN BOOKS
Printed on Carbon Captured paper

Contents

PLATFORM

THE GLOVE THIEF
BY BETH FLINTOFF

NHB

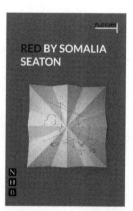

PLATFORM

RED BY SOMALIA
SEATON

NHB

PLATFORM

THE LIGHT BURNS
BLUE BY SILVA
SEMERCIYAN

NHB

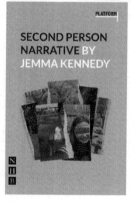

PLATFORM

SECOND PERSON
NARRATIVE BY
JEMMA KENNEDY

NHB

PLATFORM

THIS CHANGES
EVERYTHING BY
JOEL HORWOOD

NHB

PLATFORM

Commissioning and publishing a range of new plays for young actors which put girls and their stories centre stage is something I have wanted to do for a long time and, since Tonic Theatre was formed in 2011, it is an idea I have been looking to get off the ground. Tonic exists to support UK theatre to achieve greater gender equality in its workforces and its repertoires; essentially our mission is to catalyse a culture-shift in how theatre thinks and works, so that talented women are given the same levels of support and opportunity as talented men.

While it has pretty big aspirations, Tonic is a tiny organisation; we have one-and-a-bit members of staff, no core funding, and a very modest financial turnover. Because we have such limited funds and capacity, we have to use these wisely and consequently are extremely strategic about where we target our efforts. I spend much time looking to identify 'pressure points' – places where, with a bit of work, a far bigger ripple effect can be achieved. For this reason, much of our work to date has been focused on partnerships with some of the largest organisations in the country, because if they change, others will follow. But youth drama has always been clear to me as one of the greatest pressure points of all. It is the engine room of the theatre industry; tomorrow's theatre-makers (not to mention audience members) are to be found today in youth-theatre groups, university drama societies and school drama clubs all over the country.

If we can challenge their assumptions about the role of women's stories, voices, and ideas in drama, then change in the profession – in time – will be immeasurably easier to achieve.

Beyond this strategic interest in youth drama, I was convinced that girls were getting a raw deal and I found that troubling. Having worked previously as a youth-theatre director, I was familiar with the regular challenge of trying to find scripts that had adequate numbers of female roles for all the committed and talented girls that wanted to take part. In nearly all the various youth-drama groups I worked in across a five-year period, there were significantly more girls than boys. However, when it came to finding big-cast, age-appropriate plays for them to work on, I was constantly frustrated by how few there seemed to be that provided enough opportunity for the girls, its most loyal and committed participants. When looking at contemporary new writing for young actors to perform, one could be mistaken for thinking that youth drama was a predominantly male pursuit, rather than the other way round.

Aside from the practicalities of matching the number of roles to the number of girls in any one drama group, the nature of writing for female characters was something I struggled to get excited about. While there were some notable examples, often the writing for female characters seemed somewhat lacklustre. They tended to be characters at the periphery of the action rather than its heart, with far less to say and do than their male counterparts, and with a tendency towards being one-dimensional, rather than complex or vibrant, funny or surprising. Why was it that in the twenty-first century the *quality* as well as the *quantity* of roles being written for girls still seemed to lag behind those for boys so demonstrably?

Keen to check I wasn't just imagining this imbalance, Tonic conducted a nationwide research study looking into opportunities for girls in youth drama, focusing on the quantity *and* quality of roles available to them. The research was written up into a report, *Swimming in the shallow end*, and is published on the Tonic Theatre website. Not only did the research confirm my worst fears – more depressingly, it exceeded them. While many of the research participants were vocal about the social, artistic and emotional benefits that participation in youth-drama productions can have on a young person's life, so too were they – to quote the report – on 'the erosion to self-esteem, confidence and aspiration when these opportunities are repeatedly held out of reach... [and] for too many girls, this is the case'.

But despite the doom and gloom of the research findings, there remained an exciting proposition; to write stories that weren't currently being put on stage, and to foreground – rather than ignore – the experiences, achievements and world-view of young women, perhaps the group above all others in British society whose situation has altered so dramatically and excitingly over the past hundred or so years. Tonic commissioned writers I was most fascinated to see respond to the brief set to them: a large-cast play written specifically for performance by young actors, with mainly or entirely female casts and in which the female characters should be no less complex or challenging than the male characters. I asked them to write in such a way that these plays could be performed by young people anywhere in the country, and that there should be scope for every school, college and youth-theatre group performing the play to make a production their own.

At Tonic our hope is that the first Platform plays, of which this is one, will be just the beginning of a longer trajectory of work for us. Although it entails further fundraising mountains to climb, we plan to commission and publish more plays over future years. Our aspiration is that over time Platform will become a new canon of writing for young actors and one that puts girls and their lives centre stage. I dearly hope that they will be taken up by groups all over the country and performed for many years to come.

Lucy Kerbel
Director, Tonic Theatre

Acknowledgments

Tonic would like to extend its sincere thanks to:

Matt Applewhite, Tamara von Werthern, Jon Barton and all at Nick Hern Books. Moira Buffini, Kendall Masson, Matthew Poxon, Racheli Sternberg, Steph Weller. Arts Council England. The Austin and Hope Pilkington Trust. Anna Niland and the National Youth Theatre of Great Britain. Jennifer Tuckett and Central Saint Martins, Richard Williams and Drama Centre. The National Theatre Studio. English Touring Theatre.

To all the generous donors who have enabled Platform to happen. Above all to Joan Carr, who loved books, delighted in live performance, and who believed girls should never have anything less than boys.

TONIC THEATRE

Tonic Theatre was created in 2011 as a way of supporting the theatre industry to achieve greater gender equality in its workforces and repertoires. Today, Tonic partners with leading theatre companies around the UK on a range of projects, schemes, and creative works. Our groundbreaking Advance programme (www.tonictheatre-advance.co.uk) saw us work with the artistic directors and senior creative staff of a cohort of England's most influential theatres to bring about concrete change within their own organisations and the wider industry. It is a process the *Guardian* commented 'could transform the theatrical landscape forever'. *100 Great Plays for Women*, our previous collaboration with Nick Hern Books, was published in 2013 to wide acclaim and was subsequently the inspiration for a series of lectures at the National Theatre. We are now delighted to be launching Platform, our range of new plays commissioned to increase opportunity and aspiration among girls and young women who take part in youth drama.

Tonic's approach involves getting to grips with the principles that lie beneath how our industry functions – our working methods, decision-making processes, and organisational structures – and identifying how, in their current form, these can create barriers. Once we have done that, we devise practical yet imaginative alternative approaches and work with our partners to trial and deliver them. Essentially, our goal is to equip our colleagues in UK theatre with the tools they need to ensure a greater level of female talent is able to rise to the top.

Tonic is Affiliate Company at the National Theatre Studio.

www.tonictheatre.co.uk

Nick Hern Books

Theatre publishers & performing rights agents

Here at the Performing Rights Department at Nick Hern Books, we're often asked 'Are there any plays for young people?'… 'Have you got anything for a large cast?'… and 'Is there anything with strong female roles?'

Whilst the answer to these questions is, in each case, a resounding 'Yes!' (and in fact the majority of plays we've published in the last five years have been *by* women), the number of plays that fulfil all three of these criteria – strong roles for a large, predominantly or all-female cast of young actors – is less plentiful. Yet that's where there's so much demand! Nearly every teacher and youth-theatre director in the country knows that it's girls who make up the majority of their casts, and yet the plays available are often dominated by men. Because we can generally only publish what is being produced on the professional stages of the UK, until the theatre industry starts staging more plays with these qualities, the numbers will remain low. It's a vicious circle.

So with Platform, we are delighted to publish and license three plays that give young women good, strong roles to get their teeth into, and that will help them build their self-esteem and confidence in their own skills.

Nick Hern Books look after the amateur performing rights to over a thousand plays, and we know from experience that when it comes to choosing the right play it can be confusing (and pricey) to read enough of what's out there until you know which play is right for you. This is why we send out approval copies: up to three plays at a time, for thirty days, after which they have to be paid for, or returned to us in mint condition and you just need to pay the postage. So there is no reason not to read all three Platform plays to see if they will suit your school, college or youth-theatre group. We're very hopeful that one of them will.

Performing rights to the three plays will be available at a specially reduced rate to enable even those on a very tight budget to perform them. Discounts are also available on cast sets of scripts; and the cover images on these books can be supplied, free of charge, for you to use on your poster.

If you have any questions about Platform, or any of the plays on our list, or want to talk about what you're looking for, we are always happy to speak with you. Call us on 020 8749 4953, or email us at rights@nickhernbooks.co.uk.

Tamara von Werthern
Performing Rights Manager
Nick Hern Books

www.nickhernbooks.co.uk

Introduction

Joel Horwood

How do you write an introduction to a play that you would like
to speak for itself? Should I define my aims or will that limit
your ambitions? Do I give some background to the characters or
invite you to develop that for yourself? How might characters
differ between companies? How might they be similar? How
might different companies imagine daily life at The
Community? What questions might they want to ask, if not
resolve, about living on an offshore platform? What will they
decide that the platform is made of? How will they decide that
their characters grow things out here? Where might each
company decide the shore is and which shore might it be? What
will each company's interpretations of the tribal markings
actually look like? What might it be like to create your own
communal ritual? Will that affect how you feel about each other
outside a rehearsal room? Can being in a play change you for
ever? Can art ever actually change the world? Maybe I should
write about what a great and practical idea the Platform project
is? Or discuss whether the project shaped the play or
represented an opportunity to write something I had always
wanted to write? What if I asked why the play shares a title with
Naomi Klein's book? Or why these three quotations at the start
of the play? Why are they all from women I learned about
outside of school? Are we taught enough at school? Could we
be taught more? Or should we be taught how to learn and then
left to our own devices? Does everyone learn the same way? If
everyone learns the same way, how has humanity repeated so
many mistakes? Does the way we are taught shape how we see
the world? Do the stories we teach and tell affect how we see
the world? Is narrative a purely human invention to help us
make sense of chaos? Is it possible to make sense of chaos?
What's wrong with chaos? Is chaos the same as anarchy? What
is the aim of education? What could the aim of education be?

Why is it compulsory? Why does it stop? Is drama the only lesson in which there are no right answers? Which other subjects can students safely debate in without being tested? Why would anyone reduce the amount of creativity facilitated in school? Who would that serve? Is just writing a list of questions a suitable introduction to this play? Is it a play set now? Is it set here? Why not answer those in this introduction? What's the value of an unanswered question? What are you left with if you answer all of the questions? Is this play about power and control and manipulation? Is this play about hope and idealism and faith in humanity? Who wins in this play? Is it ever possible to think beyond 'winners' and 'losers'? How conditioned have we become to apply capitalist principles to every situation? Is capitalism working? What are the side effects? What would the world look like if everyone was equal? Would wars evolve? Would climate change still exist? Would we still have money? Would people still be hungry? What kind of a world would you like to live in? How could you start afresh? Is it ever possible to start afresh? What obstacles might you face? If it all collapses and fails is that the end? Or is failure part of a journey towards success? Are 'failure' and 'success' useful terms when discussing the evolution of a world-view? If we can define the world that we would like to live in, why aren't we there now? How could we change the world? Should we? Where do we start?

Acknowledgements

Maria Åberg, Rosie Armstrong, Remy Beasley, Faye Castelow, Louise Collins, Joanna Croll, Becci Gemmell, Nicola Harrison, Laura Howard, Hannah James-Scott, Lucy Kerbel, Katherine Manners, Charlotte Melia, Pippa Nixon, Rebecca Oldfield, Katherine Pearce, Eve Ponsonby, Kate Sissons, Ayse Tashkiran, Poppy Tashkiran O'Regan, Rachel Taylor, Susan Wokoma

Production Note

All of the characters are female, and should be the age of the
cast performing the play. But should your production need to
change any of these aspects then please feel free. It may also be
possible to add more characters to this play if needs be. I
suggest that these be added to the group scenes in the main to
give The Community a bigger feel. In keeping with the action
of the play, these characters should be reduced as the play draws
to a close.

THIS CHANGES EVERYTHING

'The smallest minority on Earth is the individual.
Those who deny individual rights cannot claim to be defenders
of minorities.'

Ayn Rand

'Fundamentally, the task is to articulate not just an alternative
set of policy proposals but an alternative world-view to rival the
one at the heart of the ecological crisis – embedded in
interdependence rather than hyper-individualism, reciprocity
rather than dominance, and cooperation rather than hierarchy.
… Because in the hot and stormy future we have already made
inevitable through our past emissions, an unshakable belief in
the equal rights of all people and a capacity for deep
compassion will be the only things standing between
civilisation and barbarism.'

Naomi Klein

'In my view, the only intelligence worth defending is critical,
dialectical, skeptical, desimplifying.'

Susan Sontag

Characters

in no particular order

ALVA
KLARA
KIM
MAJA
SAM
MALIN
EVE
EVIE
FREYA
TUVA
ALI
EBBA
BASIC JANE
ELIN
MOA
HENRI
AGNES
HANNE
LISA
LUCY

Setting

This play is not set here but it's set not very far from here. It's
not set now, but it's set not far from now.

The majority of the action takes place on an offshore structure
of some kind that is rusting and crumbling into the water. From
here, on a good day when the light is just right, you can almost
see the shore. But not quite. This need not be illustrated in
production but it might be important for performers to know.

ONE

The atmosphere is tense. MAJA, SAM, MALIN, FREYA,
TUVA, EVE *and* EVIE *are watching, judging* KLARA, KIM
and ALVA. *Excited, desperate to stay,* ALVA, KIM *and* KLARA
are determined to convince this strange audience to keep them.
All except KLARA, KIM *and* ALVA *bear a pseudo-tribal*
handprint mark somewhere prominent on their skin.

KLARA. We should start by saying that we followed you.

KIM. Two of you.

ALVA. In a boat.

KLARA. We followed two of you in a boat by stealing someone
else's boat.

ALVA. We didn't steal it.

KIM. But the engine wasn't very good so we lost sight of you.

KLARA. Yeah, we lost sight of your boat, you were too quick,
so then we were totally lost.

ALVA. We're gonna give the boat back.

KIM. But we kept going even when we couldn't see the shore,
we kept going.

KLARA. We thought we might run out of fuel, not be able to
get back, starve, die.

KIM. But I started rowing.

ALVA. Is this 'The Community'?

KLARA. Yeah, Kim kept rowing until we saw it, finally, this
place.

KIM. Cos we couldn't turn back, we had to get here.

ALVA. We're looking for a place called 'The Community'.

KLARA. Of course it's 'The Community', Alva, they're living in the middle of the sea!

ALVA. Right. Wow. This place is like an urban legend.

As if watching a movie, EVE *and* EVIE *open a bag of crisps and begin sharing them with each other.*

KLARA. She means that when you all disappeared, it was on the news, on the front of papers, all these theories about how you'd all just vanished. All on the same day. There were some clues, not many, but some and these rumours started, about a place called 'The Community'.

ALVA. We've been trying to find it for ages.

ALI, EBBA *and* BASIC JANE *arrive to watch.* ALVA, KLARA *and* KIM *feel the pressure.*

KIM. Klara, you'd better start at the beginning.

KLARA. Okay. So before we followed you in your boat, whoever that was, we'd basically been obsessed with those rumours for –

ALVA. For ages.

KLARA. Everyone was saying, that there was nothing to link most of you to each other. People were asking 'How did they plan this?', 'How did they communicate?', 'Where did they go?' and my dad's in the police and this is something we'd never normally do, we're not –

KIM. We photocopied some files, got your names, addresses, passwords –

KLARA. We used your social media to find people you knew, ask them stuff, and finally –

ALVA. After ages.

KLARA. Finally we started finding all these encrypted conversations which Alva decoded.

ALVA. After double ages.

KLARA. She's stubborn, Alva, she's good at codes. And what you were writing to each other about, your ideas for this place, for the world – It was addictive reading.

KIM. So by the time we found the coordinates –

ALVA. It took ages to work out that they even were coordinates.

KIM. By the time we found them, we knew, you'd actually done this.

KLARA. We thought about telling my dad, the police, your families but... we didn't.

KIM. We couldn't.

KLARA. Because we'd found you. Us. We're not exactly top of our classes, we're not cool or confident or – And we'd done it. We just knew that if we'd managed to find these bright, clever, amazing people with huge ideas –

ALVA. After ages.

KLARA. After ages, that maybe we might deserve to join.

ELIN, MOA, AGNES *and* HENRI *arrive to watch.*

KIM. We were careful. Coming here. We were really careful.

KLARA. We worked it all out. We ditched our phones so that we couldn't be tracked, avoided CCTV, changed our hair, clothes, sneaked onto the backs of trains, the ones that take cargo, we slept rough, we took a crazy route to get here just in case but we really did –

KIM. Vanish. We disappeared.

KLARA. But the coordinates were just a beach. That's all. And we couldn't go back, we didn't know what to do, we hid in a little fisherman's-hut thing, we were stuck.

ALVA. For literally ages.

KLARA. Until last night, Alva heard raised voices, shouting about 'The Community'.

KIM. She was too scared to speak to them, just woke us up.

KLARA. So when we saw two of you getting in a boat this morning –

KIM. And there was another boat, nearby –

ALVA. We borrowed it. And we're here. And we'd like to stay. Please.

KIM, KLARA and ALVA wait expectantly for a response.

It really did take ages.

KIM (*asking her to be quiet and wait for a response*). Alva.

A silence as the tribal-painted faces all look to one another.

AGNES. Ask them about Hanne.

EVIE. Shh.

All the tribal faces return to looking at ALVA, KLARA and KIM.

ALVA. Hanne? Who's Hanne? We didn't meet anyone called Hanne.

A short, tense pause while ALVA tries to think of something to say.

We didn't even meet the two people we followed. Who was that, by the way?

The tribal-painted faces all look at SAM and MAJA.

SAM. Why should we let you stay?

KIM. We saw, you've only got one boat, you can have ours.

ALVA. Our boat? It's not our boat.

SAM. There's no room for newcomers. You have to go.

KLARA. Are you in charge?

MAJA. No one's in charge.

SAM. But we can't support three more so you have to go.

TUVA. We should vote on it.

MALIN. Okay, great, everyone, thanks, now let's just hear them tell us why they should stay, okay?

Everyone looks at KLARA. *Although* KLARA *initially feels the pressure of being watched, as she speaks, she finds the lucidity of conviction, her genuine enthusiasm becoming more and more clear and inspiring.*

KLARA. We should stay because… We know why you came here. Everything back home is wrong. A few rich white men making decisions for loads of people who are not rich and white and men and those decisions are always about money while stuff's running out, people are fighting over oil, water, food – Wars are coming, riots, police violence, it's all coming unless we change how we all live, not just in little token ways but completely. We have to come up with entirely different ways of living here and what you were talking about in the conversations we decoded, fairness, equality, it all makes sense. And now we've read those, now we know all that, we don't belong back there. We can't fit in, we belong here, away from exam results, timetables, choosing what job we should do, trying to fit in to a broken system. We should stay because we can help, because we want to, because we're not just little girls, we're people and we want to change everything. With you. That's why we should stay.

KIM. And I've got a Taser.

KIM *takes out a Taser.*

For your animals. If you've got animals. Mum said it was cheaper than a cattle-prod.

KLARA. I'm sorry about Kim, she's from a broken home.

KIM. I've used it on cows before. They're pack animals, you have to let them know who's boss.

ALVA. Herd animals.

KIM. It's for when you go into the pens to kill the injured ones or males.

ALVA. Cows are herd animals.

KIM (*asking her to be quiet*). Alva.

> KLARA, KIM and ALVA *wait for a response from the group.*

MAJA. I propose that we let these arrivals eat with us and then we vote.

SAM. We can't afford to feed them.

MAJA. Have you forgotten who we are? Why we're here? I say we feed them. Who else?

> *All hands gradually go up apart from* SAM's.

> *Reluctantly,* SAM *puts her hand up.*

MALIN. This is just sooo brilliant, it's so long since I've even spoken to someone new, what were your names? Klara, Kim and...

KLARA. Alva.

MALIN. Alva. Great. So, we're gonna show you around, ask a few questions while we feed you.

MAJA. Kim can come with me.

MALIN. Brilliant, yes, thanks Maja.

ALVA. You're splitting us up?

MALIN. Showing you around, yeah, Basic Jane's with you and that leaves Klara. Now, do you like oats? Cos oats is all we've got at the moment!

> *Everyone leaves apart from* FREYA *and* TUVA. FREYA (*a panicker*), *worries at* TUVA (*who is unflappable*).

FREYA. Tuva. New people, Tuva? New people at The Community? We've never had people arrive here, ever, we've never ever been found by anyone ever before, Tuva.

TUVA. I know.

FREYA. And now, on the same day we find out Hanne's gone? I mean it's just – Isn't it? It's just – It's nuts is what it is. We do shore-runs, what once every few months now? We're phasing them out, right? And they're always to totally different coordinates, and then this time, last night, these three and – It's mental, isn't it, Tuva? It's – It's –

TUVA. Nuts.

FREYA. It's nuts, Tuva. And did you hear what they said? Did you hear what they said about following two girls in a boat, when it was three girls that left and only two came back –

TUVA. Sam and Maja.

FREYA. Sam and Maja, exactly. So what happened to Hanne, Tuva? Because, did you hear what they said? Hanne's gone, Sam and Maja are back and they heard, I'm not making this up –

TUVA. Raised voices.

FREYA. They heard raised voices, Tuva. Which means –

TUVA. Argument.

FREYA. They heard an argument, Sam and Maja didn't mention an argument, and that lot said they definitely heard an argument about – About –

TUVA. The Community.

FREYA. About The Community, Tuva. Maja, Sam and Hanne go to shore. Two of them come back after an argument? We've all been freaking out because Hanne's gone, no mention of an argument and that's – isn't it? It is a bit, right? So it's only natural that you wonder –

TUVA. What happened to Hanne.

FREYA. What if something happened to Hanne, Tuva. Maja said, didn't she? She said she left Hanne with Sam, so Sam was the last person with Hanne and now, now we know there was this – this – I mean, I'm not suggesting anything, I'm not saying anything, but just in the spirit of – of – I mean, it's just looking and sounding a bit like maybe –

TUVA. Sam did something to Hanne.

FREYA. Seriously though, I'm being serious now, Tuva, this is really serious stuff, it's like, the most serious, we don't say anything about any of this, yeah? Okay?

TUVA *takes a toke on her inhaler.*

Because, because, you know what this place is like, rumours and – and – We don't say anything, right? I mean, is that right? It's probably right isn't it, Tuva? Not to – Not to – Tuva, it's right to not talk about it, isn't it? To anyone. Isn't it? Is it?

TUVA *exhales her breath from her inhaler.*

***

BASIC JANE *is looking at something some distance from where they are stood.* ALVA *has just finished eating.*

ALVA. Thanks for the… um, what, actually, was it?

BASIC JANE. Oats… basically. And a bit of seaweed.

ALVA *tries to conceal how ill that makes her feel.*

ALVA. So… What are we doing up here?

BASIC JANE (*points*). Basically, there's a row of floats. Over there.

Pause as ALVA *waits for* BASIC JANE *to elaborate.*

ALVA. So we're here because…?

BASIC JANE. Basically… we're fishing.

A brief pause whilst ALVA *tries to think of something to say and then…*

ALVA. It's exciting, being here. Finally. Even the journey, the trains, getting lost on that boat, it was grim but… It felt a bit like shedding skin, like we were getting lighter, you know?

ALVA *waits for* BASIC JANE *to react, to say something about The Community but… she doesn't.*

Didn't expect this. In my head 'The Community' was like, a valley somewhere, not… This. What is this place? This thing we're on?

BASIC JANE. Probably an old oil rig. Sea-defence maybe. Tide-turbine. Dunno, basically.

ALVA. Has anyone else ever found The Community? Before us, I mean, because it was so hard, honestly, it's taken us, like, a year, I mean, you can't even see it from the shore and then, even from just outside, no lights, you'd never think people were actually living here, would you?

After a pause, BASIC JANE *has a really big sniff and coughs just once. She's clearly not one for small talk.*

It's sort of beautiful. The water. Sunset. Don't you think?

BASIC JANE. Yup. Basically… it's…

Pause.

…alright.

ALVA. And your boat, it's too small for all of you to fit in, how did you all get out here? Did you all arrive at different times or something? Or did you all leave from different parts of the shoreline? Or find your way here separately? Were there other coordinates or… what?

BASIC JANE. Basically… yeah.

ALVA *nods in defeat at another conversational cul-de-sac. Eventually, she tries again:*

ALVA. Why do they call you Basic Jane?

BASIC JANE. Basically…

Pause.

…they just do.

ALVA. And why did you decide to come here? What made you decide to leave everything behind and come all the way out here to this ex-power-station, metal-island, floating… thing. You've been here ages, right? I mean… Why?

Pause while BASIC JANE *thinks.*

BASIC JANE *nearly speaks but doesn't.*

Finally BASIC JANE *lands on what she has been wanting to say:*

BASIC JANE. I decided to come here when I realised that my whole life would be taken up with making tiny little choices within a massive system that was put in place way before I had any say in it. Here, I eat what I kill, I do what I want and we all want the same things, so I've stayed because there's nowhere else that I've felt more alive. Basically.

HENRI *and* AGNES *arrive.*

HENRI. Hi, new arrival, I'm Henri. This is my sister, Agnes and we have been sent to test you!

AGNES. She's gonna ask you if you like jokes –

HENRI. Do you like jokes? Before you answer, this is the test. Jokes? Course you like them! Test passed! Fun-guns set to HILARIOUS! Ready? How many immature people does it take to change a light bulb?… YOUR MUM!

No reaction.

Moving on. Can I ask exactly what you heard during that argument?

AGNES. Would you recognise their voices? Did you hear any names?

ALVA. I didn't hear much, to be honest.

HENRI. Don't worry, you're not in trouble, just, did they seem like they knew each other or –

ALVA. Think they knew each other.

HENRI. Okay and you didn't hear how the argument ended? No one mentioned leaving or running away or anything violent –

ALVA. No, I didn't hear much at all, definitely nothing violent.

HENRI. Okay, cool. Well, we will see you at the group meeting later on. Come on, sissy pops.

HENRI *leaves*, AGNES *rolls her eyes and diligently follows her sister.*

ALVA. Why is she asking if I heard anything violent? Is there something going on here?

BASIC JANE. Basically, Hanne's gone missing.

ALVA. Who's Hanne?

***

EVE, EVIE, MALIN *and* MAJA *are with* KIM. KIM *is eating a bowl of oats.*

MAJA. Hanne started the forums, bought the boat, she discovered this place.

EVIE. The meeting room?

EVE. She means The Platform.

KIM. What's The Platform?

MALIN. It's great, is what it is! It's what we call this whole structure, up top it's got open space, we've started to grow things, some of the rooms are even below sea level, it's awesome –

MAJA. Anyway! Really it was Hanne who started The Community.

EVIE. She knew how to work the power.

EVE. She was the only person who knew how to work the power.

KIM. And now she's gone?

MALIN. *Right now*, she's gone. But that might not mean she's gone for ever.

MAJA. But it is why we're asking you about the argument you overheard.

MALIN. They said raised voices, not 'argument'.

EVE. They said 'scared'.

EVIE. Was there screaming?

MAJA. We just want to know exactly what you overheard, that's all.

KIM. Do you think someone hurt Hanne? Deliberately?

MALIN, EVE and EVIE look to MAJA for an answer.

MAJA. Is that the kind of thing you overheard?

SAM. No one did anything to Hanne.

Unseen, SAM has been overhearing this.

We can't trust her. She followed us, now she's saying someone hurt Hanne? She's lying.

MAJA. Why would she lie, Sam?

SAM. Ask her that. If anyone did something to Hanne, it's most likely her.

KIM. I don't even know who Hanne is!

SAM. You're not welcome here, you take your boat and you leave.

MAJA. Sam, calm down.

SAM. *We* all work to make this place. *All* of us. *Us*. Not them. It's The Code.

MAJA. Sam! We have got this under control.

SAM pushes past KIM and leaves, KIM is shaken.

Sorry about her. She can just be a bit...

EVE. Scary.

EVIE. She's mental.

KIM. I promise, I didn't do anything, I wouldn't.

MAJA. It's okay.

KIM. We just loved the idea of this place, saw your boat, followed and – and – found you all.

MAJA. She's just trying to blame you.

EVE. Yeah.

EVIE. She is.

MALIN. Is she?

MAJA. Sam's been acting a little strangely for a while.

EVE. Yeah.

EVIE. She has.

EVE. She's paranoid.

EVIE. She's mental.

EVE. Maja's the only one who stands up to her.

MALIN. Okay great, guys, but remember The Code? We've got a vote to prepare for.

KIM. Code? What code?

***

EBBA. The Code is the whole idea but in three, sort of, rules.

ALI is struggling with plugs and extension leads. EBBA is gesticulating with a pair of rubber gloves to help her story, she wants KLARA to love this place. KLARA is hungrily finishing her oats.

We were all frustrated and, sort of, angry, you saw our conversations, we met online in forums about protests and activism, we all wanted to change things.

KLARA. What did you want to change?

EBBA. All of it. Sort of, everything. The whole system has to change because it's all connected. Rich people convince other people to use more stuff, so the stuff starts running out, so the price goes up, so wars start and the planet warms up because all the stuff is, sort of, being used up. And it started as, sort of, a good idea, that system. The idea that if everyone is, sort of, in competition with each other then all of us try our best so everything will always, sort of, get better. But that isn't happening. We need a new idea.

KLARA. And The Code is the new idea?

EBBA. Sort of. Before, online, as a, sort of, game we started to invent our own idea by working out what's, sort of, important to each of us. Just in conversations we worked out sort of –

ALI. Ebba, where are the gloves?

EBBA. Worked out that we all wanted to pitch in, we didn't want there to be money, we wanted time for meetings to discuss the big things, we wanted everyone included in, sort of, everything. But then you'd leave these *brilliant* conversations and you'd go to school and, sort of, just hate how the real world was nothing like this, sort of, amazing community we were imagining, until, Hanne was like… 'Why don't we, sort of, do this?'

ALI (*taking the gloves from* EBBA's *hands*). Thank you.

Without breaking stride, EBBA *picks up an extension lead to gesticulate with instead.*

EBBA. But none of us wanted it to be, sort of, an extended camping trip. If we really wanted to invent a new idea, it couldn't be just, sort of, for us. It had to be for everyone, sort of, everywhere. So, we figured that, if it worked, without money, without 'isms' or politics –

ALI. Ebba, where's the extension cord?

EBBA. We could tell people, 'this is not a theory, we've literally really actually, sort of, done this and it definitely works' –

ALI. Extension cord?

EBBA. What extension cord?

ALI *(taking the extension lead from* EBBA*'s hand)*. Thank you.

EBBA. Where was I?

KLARA. The Code.

EBBA. Yeah, so, when we arrived, after putting money we'd saved in a kitty for supplies, we, sort of, started working on The Code. We wanted really clear, simple rules for how we'd all, sort of, be here. So we spent days, sort of, discussing and debating until we got it down to three rules that –

ALI. 'The Community Is The Individual, The Individual Is The Community.'

EBBA. The Community is the individual, the individual is The Community. We're all connected. Everyone has to agree on everything that happens here. Which means there are loads of meetings but also, there are no, sort of, minorities. And the second rule is…

   EBBA *picks up a screwdriver to gesticulate with but* ALI *holds out her hand.*

ALI. 'We All Work To Make This Place.'

   EBBA *puts the screwdriver in* ALI*'s hand.*

EBBA. We all work to make this place, so equal shifts, fishing, cooking, cleaning. But it also sort of means that we know it takes work to stay here. The hard stuff is important.

KLARA. Hard stuff like…?

EBBA. Well, chores, obviously but also the meetings, they are, sort of, endless. And there's a meeting later on, actually, so we'd better make sure there's power, Ali.

Bored of being the only one actually working, ALI *starts hitting something to try to make it work.*

We don't actually know how any of this, sort of, works by the way. We're just, sort of, trying some stuff out. We get shocks, hence the gloves. It's all, sort of, redirecting power, trial and error.

ALI *returns to plugging and unplugging plugs.*

ALI. Get on with the third rule and then give me a hand!

EBBA (*rolling her eyes*). The third rule is about trying every possibility, listening to each other –

ALI. The third rule is 'There Are No Bad Answers'.

EBBA (*sarcastic*). Thank you, Ali! Anyway, we all came here because we didn't, sort of, know the answers. And if you're trying to do something totally new then you don't know if any possible answers are, sort of, good or bad, until you try them. It's all, sort of, part of the process, even the bad answers, so the bad answers aren't actually, sort of, bad.

ALI *plugs something in and something makes a weird noise.*

ALI. NO! No no no no…

ALI *unplugs whatever it was.*

KLARA. What about the handprints? The markings on your faces?

EBBA (*glowing*). These? I love these! They were Ali's idea. We were really, sort of, excited about being here and having actually finally really become The Community that we'd been talking about so we wanted a way to, sort of, not celebrate but, it's hard to explain. We wanted a sort of ritual, about relying on each other, we all repaint these daily to remind us but the ritual was –

ALI. If she stays, she's gonna have to do it.

EBBA. Totally! And the cleansing-the-past-type thing, jumping in the sea or a water fight, then we each marked one other person, so someone will mark you because, it's, sort of, about –

ALI. Being a tribe.

MOA and ELIN arrive.

ELIN. Is the power working?

EBBA. Oh, come on, we've been working our fingers to the bone in here! Give us a break!

ELIN. Okay, well, it's time for the meeting.

KLARA. What's the meeting about?

MOA. It's about you.

***

Everyone, except for those in the previous scene, is watching MAJA and SAM, mid-argument.

SAM. They can't stay! There's no way this place can take three more people. Besides, if Hanne's gone then it's all over, it hasn't worked, we should go home.

MAJA. What makes you think she won't come back?

SAM. Because she's gone! She didn't meet us at the boat, she just left. Hanne is no more! It's home-time for everyone, game over, this place is finished.

MAJA. Why would you say that?

MOA, ELIN, KLARA, ALI and EBBA arrive and watch.

SAM. The plan was to test ideas out, she tested them and bailed. Had her fill of meetings, of oats, of being freezing cold and she just left. Can you blame her?

ELIN. I am so sick of eating oats.

MOA. Me too.

SAM. Hanne's the one who started all of it, if even she's gone, face it, it's over.

AGNES. Are we all going home?

MAJA. Why would you say that 'Hanne is no more'? What do you mean?

SAM. What?

MAJA. How long have you wanted The Community to end?

SAM. I don't want it to end.

MAJA. You just said you're sick of this place.

SAM. I'm sick of being cold and eating bad food, so is everyone else.

MAJA. Would you have said all this if Hanne was here?

SAM. Course I would, it's true.

MAJA. I left Hanne with you at the boat, didn't I, Sam?

SAM. Yeah, then she went looking for you.

MAJA. So when did the argument happen?

SAM. What?

EVE. Was it her?

EVIE. Were you arguing with Hanne?

SAM. No, of course I wasn't!

MAJA. You didn't expect us to be followed, did you? Didn't expect there to be witnesses. That's why you've never wanted these new arrivals here, isn't it?

SAM. You seriously think I hurt her?

MAJA. I don't feel safe here with you, Sam. I propose a vote, either we all leave or Sam does.

Furious, SAM *makes to attack* MAJA *but* KIM *stands in* SAM's *way, Taser in hand.*

KIM. Sam, you stay away, for the good of the herd.

ALVA. Pack.

KIM (*telling her to be quiet*). Alva.

MAJA. Who thinks Sam should leave?

All hands go up except for those of the new arrivals and
SAM.

Then KIM*'s hand goes up. And then* KLARA*'s.*

No one wants you here, Sam.

SAM *seems like she's about to explode with rage at* MAJA,
but KIM *still stands between them with her Taser.*

SAM (*indicating* KLARA, KIM *and* ALVA). I'm taking the
boat you stole and giving it back because I'm good. I never
did anything to anyone. I really liked Hanne. If something
happened to her, it'll happen again. Bad things are gonna
happen here. It's over.

SAM *leaves.*

HENRI. That was awkward.

MAJA *can feel the mood is low, she wants people to stay so
must think on her feet.*

MAJA. It was awkward because she's right. She said some
things we agree with. It is cold, the food's bad, and we're not
doing anything about it. Bad things are going to happen here
if we've forgotten how to change things. But what do we do
when we want change? We talk about it, we have a meeting,
do nothing. We're so busy being equal that we pretend that
some people aren't just better at some things. Freya and Tuva
are brilliant electricians, if we stopped worrying about equal
chores and let them fix some of the old heaters, things *would*
get warmer.

TUVA *takes a toke on her inhaler.*

Henri's food is amazing, if we did her other chores for her,
she could cook for all of us, the food *would* get better. We
could all leave now in the only boat we've got or we could
try one last time to make this place amazing with less
talking, more doing.

AGNES. But how do we decide what to do without meetings?

MAJA. We delegate. Someone keeps an eye on the big picture, while everyone else gets on with the important things, like a manager, calling meetings when necessary.

EBBA. Isn't that against The Code? Having a leader?

MAJA. Can The Code not change? Shouldn't we try out other ideas?

MALIN. Great, brilliant, no bad answers, let's try a leader for maybe a week or something and –

AGNES. And if it doesn't work, we go home?

BASIC JANE. But if it does, we can vote for a new leader, basically, trial periods.

MALIN. Cool, yeah, okay, so in a week, if the leader thing hasn't worked, home-time, yeah?

KIM. I vote Maja should be leader for the week.

MALIN. Brilliant, totally getting stuck in, who else votes that Maja be the leader for a week?

Everyone votes for MAJA.

HENRI. For one week, The Community is The Leader, The Leader is The Community!

MAJA. And as your leader, I command that we welcome our new arrivals!

EVE *and* EVIE *start to chant: 'The Community is The Leader, The Leader is The Community!' The chant grows into a joyous and silly tribal ritual full of music.*

Under MAJA's *instructions,* KLARA, KIM *and* ALVA *are jostled into position and are ceremonially, ritualistically, beautifully marked into The Community with a handprint. For once, we see The Community functioning perfectly. Here, among the celebrations,* KLARA, KIM *and* ALVA *discover the feeling that they have been searching for.*

A feeling that, for once, they are an important part of something, for once, they belong; here, they have finally found a real home.

If The Code is written somewhere visible, MALIN *rewrites the first rule to read: 'The Community is The Leader, The Leader is The Community.'*

TWO

One week later.

TUVA *and* FREYA *are warming their hands near an electric heater.*

FREYA. Today's the day, Tuva. Big day today. Big vote, Tuva. First meeting in ages. In how long? Ages, Tuva, am I wrong? First meeting in ages, literally, like –

TUVA. A week.

FREYA. Exactly, Tuva. First meeting in a whole week. How weird is that!? So used to having meetings all the time and now, it's been ages since we've all sat around, talking, listening arguing about everything, when it's actually only been –

TUVA. A week.

FREYA. Nuts. Mad. Nuts and mad that it's only been a week when so much has changed! It's not as if it'll be a close one, is it? Not as if anyone's gonna vote to go back to how it was before when it's obvious that Maja's turned things around, it's so obvious, Tuva, isn't it? So obvious that literally everyone, everyone is gonna vote for –

TUVA. I'm not.

FREYA. What?

TUVA *takes a toke on her inhaler.*

You don't want Maja to be leader? What are you voting for instead, Tuva, going home? Leaving? Leaving, Tuva, when we've finally got the heat going and Elin and Moa have sussed out how to grow more stuff, you're gonna – gonna – What are you gonna do?

TUVA (*exhaling*). Vote to leave.

FREYA. Leave, Tuva? Why would you leave? What are you – ? What are you – ? Are you – !?

TUVA. Always said we would.

FREYA. Yeah, no, yeah, we did, but no, though. No. We said, right? We said, we'd go home, yeah? Once we'd worked out how to all be, be, and that's this. That's now. Because before, yeah? Before, what were we gonna tell people back home, that it was, you know, it was, cold and – and – That's what we were – That's what we – Isn't it? It is. But now, these ideas, skills, now we're getting somewhere, you can't – Can't vote to – Are you – ? Tuva? Are you messing? Hey? Humour, you are so, aren't you? You are. You're so, aren't you? Dry. You are, ever so dry, humour I mean, sense of, it's dry, isn't it?

TUVA. It was working before. All this is just… nicer.

FREYA. No – Yeah – No – I mean – I mean – I me– N– Ye– unh… Just… What?

MALIN *arrives*.

MALIN. Brilliant, here you are, the meeting's about to start, okay?

FREYA. But, what about, Eve and Evie? They're not back from the – the – are they?

MALIN. Maja sent them further afield, this time. They'll be back soon, I'm sure.

FREYA. But, a shore-run? Why another shore-run so soon? Aren't they every few months? And –

MALIN. Honestly, I'm not totally in the loop on this one, I just know that on the last shore-run, when Sam attacked Hanne, they didn't come back with much.

TUVA. Just crisps.

MALIN. Just quite a lot of crisps, yeah. Now, can you help gather people for the meeting or do you need to stay beside your fancy new heater?

***

HENRI *and* AGNES *are with* BASIC JANE, ELIN *and* MOA. *Standing around a strange object, shivering.*

BASIC JANE. Basically, they work.

ELIN. Obviously, they work.

MOA. We knew the traps would work.

AGNES. But… Do we really want to start eating seagulls?

MOA (*dubious*). Yeah.

HENRI. Start? Do you even know what was in the curry last night?

ELIN. You what?

AGNES. She's joking.

HENRI. I'm joking!

AGNES. Once your traps catch a seagull… Who kills it? And gets the feathers off and… whatever.

MOA. Yeah, who's gonna do that?

ELIN. I'm not doing it.

BASIC JANE. I'm basically fine with it.

HENRI. You kill them, I'll cook them, everyone's happy.

ELIN. Especially you, in your toasty kitchen.

MOA. So toasty.

ELIN. Might be time to shift some of the roles soon, you know.

MOA. Agreed.

AGNES. If we stay here.

MOA. *If* we stay here?

HENRI. Things are just starting to get better, we're totally staying.

MOA. Yeah, everyone's gonna vote to stay, right?

ELIN. Obviously! Maja's been amazing, things are so much better, we're all voting to stay.

BASIC JANE. Basically... I'm not.

AGNES. You're gonna vote to leave?

MOA. Why would you vote to leave?

ELIN. It's only been a week, imagine what it'd be like in two or a month?

MOA. It'd be amazing!

HENRI. If you think we should leave why bother working on seagull traps in the first place?

BASIC JANE. Basically... we always said we'd take new ideas back home.

MOA (*dubious*). Eating seagulls?

HENRI. No bad answers, everyone's entitled to their own – But why would we leave now!?

BASIC JANE. The whole point was basically to go back, otherwise, who are we helping?

ELIN. The plan was only to go back when we had the best possible idea totally worked out.

MOA. Which isn't this.

ELIN. Not yet, anyway.

BASIC JANE. But isn't this basically just more comfy?

HENRI. Yeah, whilst still being totally equal, totally brilliant and totally a new thing.

ELIN. It's way better.

MOA. And personally, I just really like it here now.

FREYA *and* TUVA *arrive, slightly out of breath.*

FREYA. So, you've got to come cos the big meeting's started the one with the vote and it's started so you've got to come, but, also, someone's got to find and tell the new arrivals as well.

TUVA *points at* BASIC JANE.

***

KIM *is trying to get past* KLARA *and* ALVA.

KLARA. No, Kim, this time we have to talk.

KIM. I'm working –

ALVA. You've been avoiding us all week.

KIM. I've been making schedules with Maja.

KLARA. You almost Tasered someone, Kim!

KIM. I helped!

KLARA. We don't know these people, we just arrived and you threatened to Taser someone.

KIM. I'm the reason they let us stay.

KLARA. People are scared of you, I'm having to be extra-double nice just to prove I'm not all up for threatening violence. Who brings a Taser to a peaceful community!?

KIM. I did it for all of us! I thought you knew me, I thought you'd know that.

KLARA. We should be making friends not scaring everyone with a Taser.

ALVA. Why did you vote that Sam should leave?

KLARA. Alva, how is that relevant?

ALVA. We only heard voices, why did you vote Sam out?

KLARA. Because she was a psycho! But that doesn't mean Kim should threaten people.

KIM. Would you rather I hadn't got involved? Would you rather the whole place fell apart as soon as we arrived? I took some responsibility, maybe you should start doing the same.

ALVA. How? It's just the same as back home, there's a leader and some followers.

KLARA. We voted against Sam to make this place better, can we talk about Kim now, please?

ALVA. I didn't leave everything behind to just sit up there and do a job.

KIM. We all work for each other. Me and Maja have been working for you as much as you've been working for us. And if you can't see that then, then I really can't tell why we ever became friends in the first place.

BASIC JANE *arrives*.

BASIC JANE. Basically, where have you been? I've basically been looking for you lot for basically the entire meeting! Come on or they'll have basically sorted out all the basics without us.

***

Most of The Community are gathered for the meeting. Only EVE and EVIE and those from the previous scene are missing. MAJA stands in the centre.

MALIN. Great, okay, brilliant. Lovely to be back in the meeting room with everyone again. Just to say, Maja called this meeting so we could all work out where to go from here. I think we'd all agree, sterling work by everyone this past week. Particularly Ali and Ebba with the power, Henri with the cooking, Freya and Tuva with the heat. Loving your work. Amazing. But, most of all, the woman who made it all happen, our leader, Maja.

MALIN *starts a round of applause*. MAJA *accepts it gracefully before quieting it down*.

MAJA. It has been an honour to work for The Community this past week. We made great progress. But we agreed, today, we would vote on whether we stay or find a new leader.

BASIC JANE, ALVA, KLARA *and* KIM *arrive.*

So, how best to do this? Shall we first vote on whether or not we'll stay here? All those –

EVE. STOP!!

EVE *and* EVIE *arrive. Breathless from running.*

EVIE. Yeah, stop.

EVE. Everyone stop!

HENRI. We've stopped.

MALIN. You haven't missed the vote, just take a seat and –

EVE. No, it's news.

EVIE. News.

EVE. News from shore.

EVIE. We've got news from the shore.

MALIN. What happened?

EVE. War.

EVIE. World war.

MAJA. A world war?

EVE. There's a whole massive world war happening.

EVIE. In the world.

AGNES. What are they saying? What are you saying – You mean –

ALVA. A world war!?

Someone screams, everyone starts to panic and shout.

ELIN. What if there's a nuclear bomb, Malin?

MOA. Bombs, Malin!

ELIN. Or airborne chemical weapons?

MALIN. Everyone stay calm.

ELIN. If there's a war, how are we gonna get supplies!?

MOA. An actual war?

MALIN. Okay, everyone stay calm!

HENRI. We need a phone, we need to know what's happening.

MALIN. No one's got any phones here, you know that!

KIM. EVERYONE JUST SHUT UP!!

Everyone falls silent.

MALIN. Thanks Kim, um, okay, so, Maja gave me the job
     before of – of helping people get on, so let's try to treat this
     like a meeting and listen and, right, Maja? We should just…
     Oh, God.

KLARA. Just tell us what you saw. Tell us how you know this.

EVIE. Um… I saw… Fires. And… Bodies. Got to the town and
     there were fires. And bodies. Doors open. Windows smashed.
     And this sound like a humming sound but from high up. Like
     having the TV on in a different room. And then, far away but
     not that far away, this rushing sound and explosions.
     Everything smelled like burned meat. There was no one.
     Like a film. There was a radio. We listened to it and it said
     'war'.

KLARA. But what happened? Did they say how or what?

EVIE. Terrorists.

EVE. Climate change.

EVIE. Climate-change terrorists.

EVE. Whole cities have gone.

ALVA. What do you mean 'gone'?

EVIE. Power stations. They attacked power stations. Nuclear ones. Other governments retaliated, countries fired weapons and now there's clouds of poison everywhere.

ALVA. What about place names, did you hear any actual place names?

KLARA. When you say everywhere, do you mean this has happened all over the world or – ?

EVE. EVERYWHERE! Everyone. They were nuclear explosions. Sorry.

KLARA *starts to cry.*

EVIE. We got scared and we came back with everything we could.

ALVA. Clouds of poison?

ALI. Radioactive rain, I've read about radioactive rain.

EVIE. Yeah.

ALVA. We should go to shore and find out the facts, we should send other people, I'll go.

KIM. Shh, Alva.

EVE. If you want to take the boat and see for yourself then go ahead.

MALIN. But if there's radioactive rain? If it's a war zone – No one should leave.

ALVA. But this changes everything!

MAJA. It changes nothing.

MAJA *finally stands up.*

There is a war over there. But not here. Here, we're growing and catching food. We have power, heat. No one knows we're here. There is nowhere safer in the entire world –

BASIC JANE. If this is basically the safest place around, shouldn't we bring other people here?

ELIN. No. Radiation poisoning?

MOA. No way.

EBBA. You want this to be a, sort of, refugee camp!?

BASIC JANE. I'm basically just saying –

MAJA. If I could finish?

BASIC JANE. Yeah, basically, course you can, yeah.

MAJA. As I was saying, we have all we need. Everything can easily be counted and rationed. We can work a watch into the rotas to keep an eye on the shore for any sign of danger or change. But we don't need rumours about this stuff, so for our peace of mind, those watches should just talk to the leader about whatever they see. What do you think?

EVE. I think you should stay as leader.

EVIE. Me too.

FREYA. You've done really well at it, so you should stay as leader, yeah.

MAJA *looks around The Community but no one seems interested in having a vote on the matter.*

MAJA. Okay. Well, people like Ali and Ebba have proved that we can survive together. Solving problems like the power are more important now than ever before. We've always said 'We All Work Together To Make This Place', if the last week is anything to go by, then I think we'd all agree that actually; work makes this place.

HENRI. Work makes this place.

AGNES. Is there really no way I can call home?

KLARA. What for, Agnes!? Even if there was a phone, if there was any signal, what's the point!?

ALVA *hugs* KLARA.

AGNES. I just want to see if they're okay.

MAJA. Agnes, let's talk this through. You want to call home to see if they're okay.

AGNES. Yeah.

MAJA. And if they're not, what then?

AGNES. Don't know.

MAJA. And if they are, what then?

AGNES. Don't know.

MAJA. So if there was a phone and you found out whatever you want to find out. And if every computer on the planet is scouring the world for targets, and they found a signal from your phone, coming from a place that isn't on any maps, close to the mainland, with people on it. Do you think we might look a little bit like a target? Do you think we'd hear the bombs? Do you think you'd hear people saying, 'Even though it's cost us our lives, I'm glad little Agnes found out that her parents were... dot dot dot'?

AGNES. Sorry.

MAJA. Do you want us to survive this, Agnes?

AGNES. Yes.

MAJA. Then maybe you should stop thinking about yourself and start thinking about the group. Because really, this is proof. It proves we were right. The system back there led to war. Here, we're making something new. We're making a new and better home. Yeah?

AGNES. Yeah. I do think of this place as home. Sorry, everyone.

MAJA. Now, I've got work to do. You can all stay here talking if you want.

MAJA *leaves. Gradually everyone else leaves too; all comforting each other. If The Code is written somewhere visible,* MALIN *changes it from 'We All Make This Place Work' to 'Work Makes This Place'.*

After everyone has left, EVE *opens a new packet of crisps and starts eating.*

EVIE. What do you think?

EVIE *takes a crisp and eats it.*

Eve, what do you think?

EVIE *takes a crisp and eats it.*

What are you thinking, Eve?

EVIE *takes a crisp and eats it.*

EVE. I'm thinking, I don't like it. Let's give it until the crisps run out and then... We should go.

EVE *scrunches the bag up and puts it in her pocket.*

THREE

Some weeks later.

FREYA. Gone!? Gone, Tuva, just, I mean, just gone? Gone gone or gone like – ? No, just – That's not – I mean, when you say 'gone', what do you mean?

TUVA. The boat's gone.

FREYA. Okay, okay, the boat's, okay, it's gone, Tuva, so that's, that's, isn't it? 'Gone' as in it's gone somewhere as in someone took it and they'll bring it back so that's fine or 'gone' as in, now we've got no boats, Tuva, as in the only boat we had is actually really totally –

TUVA. The boat's gone.

FREYA. Why is the boat gone!? We don't do shore-runs with the war on, everyone's been doing shift work every day for weeks, Tuva, no one uses the boat but you're saying, are you saying this? You're saying the boat is gone for ever and we've got no boats, Tuva, is that –

TUVA. The boat's... (*Instead of finishing her sentence,* TUVA *takes a toke on her inhaler.*)

FREYA. Gone, the boat's gone, gone is the boat, Tuva, it's gone, no boat, no boat, just us on The Platform in the middle of the sea with no boat, being completely actually, Tuva, STUCK!?

MALIN *arrives.*

MALIN. Hey guys, hi, great work on the watch tonight, just got to let you know that we've had a couple of technical hitches with the power downstairs, Ali and Ebba worked through the night to make sure we still had... Actually, is everything okay, you both seem a bit...?

TUVA *finally exhales.*

TUVA. We need to speak to Maja.

***

BASIC JANE *is looking at something some distance from where they are stood.* ALVA *is prodding something on the ground with a stick.*

ALVA. They're so thick. Ants. Ants are soooo thick. This one. This one here, has actually been trying to fit this little twig through this little tiny hole for… ages. All day practically.

Pause.

BASIC JANE. Ants basically have the most sophisticated social organisation of anything on the planet.

ALVA. What?

BASIC JANE. It's science, basically.

ALVA. Well, this one's not sophisticated, this one's a stupid thick dumb idiot ant with no brains.

Pause.

BASIC JANE. Ants aren't clever, but, basically, the group is. It's in their genes to perform these basic roles so that, basically, the group survives. That's what 'sophisticated' means really, just that they're organised so well that they'll just keep on, basically, surviving, for ages.

Pause.

ALVA. What kind of roles?

BASIC JANE. Each group has a queen. Some males. Lots of workers, basically.

Pause.

ALVA. What do the males do?

BASIC JANE. Mate with the queen. Die.

Pause.

ALVA. What do the queens do?

BASIC JANE. Have babies. Basically. Which means she's working a lot.

ALVA. But, she doesn't run things.

BASIC JANE. None of them do.

Pause.

ALVA. None of them know what they're doing or why, and that's sophisticated?

BASIC JANE. Basically, yeah.

Pause.

ALVA. What do the workers do?

BASIC JANE. Everything. Find food, build stuff, protect it, basically, keep it going no matter what.

ALVA. So, how is moving that twig what this ant was genetically programmed to do? How is that ant helping the colony?

BASIC JANE. It's performing its role. Even if it's a stupid one. Basically, if any of the ants gave up and wandered off, the rest of the workers would chase it and kill it.

ALVA. For working out that it's a pointless job, the stick's too big?

BASIC JANE. Because any worker who threatens the system, threatens the existence of the whole colony. If that ant wasn't there, doing its stupid job, the others might decide that they should stop too. Next thing you know, nothing gets done and the whole thing, basically, just collapses, end of colony, end of species, basically, the whole lot has to start again.

ALVA *watches the ant.*

ALVA *kills the ant.*

Pause.

MALIN *arrives.*

MALIN. Okay, community meeting, guys, let's go.

ALVA. What about the nets and the bird traps? Someone needs to be watching these basically –

MALIN. This one's important, Alva.

ALVA. But so's catching food, aren't these basically our roles, shouldn't we basically be –

MALIN. Okay! Alva! Community meeting. Thank you.

***

ALI *and* EBBA *have finished eating two bowls of food and are passing another between them.* AGNES *and* HENRI *are at a slight distance, watching.*

AGNES. It's my food.

EBBA. No, Agnes. Run me through your opinion of The Code, because it's, sort of, really clear to me. We're working towards a, sort of, fairer society, aren't we? And it must be fairer that those who contribute more, get more back, mustn't it? Doesn't that sound fair?

AGNES. That's my breakfast ration.

EBBA. It, sort of, doesn't make any sense that you'd even argue about this. Henri, you're the cook, your sister's clearly not getting a, sort of, grip on this one. Help us explain.

HENRI. She's younger than you.

ALI. So?

HENRI. So, you should give it back.

EBBA. I'm, sort of, too tired for this, actually. Agnes, you just don't work as hard as we do, it's sort of, a fact. It's really clear, it's in The Code, work makes this place.

AGNES. I work.

ALI. You're the cleaner.

AGNES. I do some cleaning, that doesn't make me the cleaner.

EBBA. Agnes, we're in charge of power. We make sure this entire platform has power. We were up all night keeping the power going. What were you doing? Sort of, cleaning?

ALI. Don't bother, Ebba.

EBBA. Look, I'm bothering because I want to give you a say in everything, Agnes. I'm keeping us firmly within, sort of, grasp of what we're doing here but surely, you can see it makes sense. Surely, you can see that it's only fair.

HENRI. If you want more rations, speak to Malin about it, she can talk to Maja for you.

EBBA. We don't need to talk to anyone, we agreed, fewer meetings. It's nice to have, sort of, clean things but what would you choose, shiny surfaces or *electricity*? Because all this, in here, is, sort of, what we do. This is why our hands constantly stink of rubber gloves, we risk electric shocks –

AGNES. You only plug things in. That's what Henri says, she says you only plug things in.

ALI. 'Plug things in'?

HENRI. It was a joke, I make jokes.

ALI. Do you have any idea how horrible it is in the engine room? How hard I work?

EBBA. We work so hard for you, Agnes. And you're making, sort of, jokes about us? From your lovely kitchen with all that lovely food that you dole into little, sort of, rations?

ALI. I bet they lick the bowl, skim a bit off the top.

EBBA. And then act as if we're the ones, sort of, breaking The Code.

AGNES. Taking my food is against The Code!

ALI. Work Makes This Place. Not cleaning, work. Real work. Power.

EBBA. More important now than ever before. There's a war on, Agnes. You're doing a good thing by donating your food to us.

AGNES. If you don't stop this, one day, I'll –

KIM *arrives,* HENRI *covers.*

HENRI. – Enjoy eating out again some time? Me too, little sis. Hi, Kim, didn't see you there.

KIM *looks at each of them in turn.*

KIM. There's a meeting. Everyone needs to be there.

***

ELIN *and* MOA *are fiddling with one of their inventions.* KLARA *watches them.*

ELIN. I miss bad TV most.

MOA. Saturday mornings.

ELIN. Bad TV on Saturday mornings!

MOA. Where people just talk about stuff.

ELIN. And someone sings a song and someone cooks something.

MOA. And then they talk about what they were talking about before again.

ELIN. I miss all that so much.

KLARA. Don't you miss your families?

ELIN. We're working, Klara.

MOA. Yeah, let us focus, Klara.

ELIN. Course we miss our families.

MOA. Course we do.

ELIN. Not all of them.

MOA. Not my mum.

ELIN. My brother was too young to have done anything wrong. He wouldn't even join cadets because of all the shouting. But not home. I don't miss home.

MOA. I miss selling stuff on the internet.

ELIN. These things would have sold so much, these freshwater-traps?

MOA. No, but seriously, we could sell these for loads.

ELIN. We would be minted.

MOA. Two houses at least.

ELIN. At least.

MOA. And a pool. And a chocolate fountain. A massive flat-screen TV for Saturday mornings.

KLARA. So, you don't think about leaving?

MOA. Leaving? No.

ELIN. Why ask that?

MOA. Yeah, why ask?

ELIN. We've told you before about interrupting while we're working.

MOA. You're supposed to be assisting us.

ELIN. I can't concentrate now.

MOA. You're supposed to be learning this stuff from us.

ELIN. Are you spying on us or something?

KLARA. 'Spying'? No.

ELIN. Checking up on us and reporting to Maja?

KLARA. No!

ELIN. Don't think we haven't noticed that you're one of her favourites.

KLARA. Maja hates me.

MOA. You're one of her favourites.

ELIN. Getting this job, in the warm, hardly any shifts out in the cold, you're in the inner circle, you are, same as Kim, same as Malin.

KLARA. I'm not spying.

MOA. You're best friends with Kim, aren't you?

ELIN. Shut up, Moa.

KLARA. I was, I never see her any more, what's that got to do with anything?

ELIN. No one's saying anything about Kim.

MOA. Because she'd kill anyone who does.

ELIN. Shut up!

KIM *arrives*.

MOA *and* ELIN *work really hard for a moment, pretending they haven't been talking*.

KIM. There's a meeting. We all need to be there.

***

Everyone from The Community is present for the emergency meeting except for those in the previous scene.

MALIN. Great but really, so what? The boat's gone. Work makes this place, we just carry on.

EBBA. But we can't get to shore for screws, extension cord –

MALIN. Cool, but maybe this is an opportunity, you know? The plan was always to phase out the shore-runs, to be self-sufficient. We've managed so far, what else do we really need?

BASIC JANE. Basically, we really need to talk to Maja.

MALIN. Maja's busy, besides you know it's my responsibility to handle things like this.

ALVA. We don't need handling, we need a new boat.

MALIN. Okay, cool, but honestly, we haven't needed a boat for over a month now, and we're managing pretty well, wouldn't you say?

FREYA. I don't want us to have to, you know, manage, that's not what this idea is about.

ALVA. What is this idea about?

EBBA. It's about being successful!

KLARA, MOA, ELIN *and* KIM *arrive.*

KIM. We gathered everyone to find out if anyone saw Eve and Evie take the boat?

FREYA. Okay, so, no, but it was our watch, but because it was our watch, we were up in the – the, weren't we, Tuva? To watch the shoreline from up in the, and – and – you know, normal, watch, from up in the, bit cold, so, thought we'd have a little, go on a little – just to – to – And that's when we saw, or rather, we didn't, then Malin and here and that's what happened.

KIM. And who was the last person to see them? Eve and Evie, who saw them last?

HENRI. I saw them at dinner last night, just eating crisps and being normal.

AGNES. Why would they leave?

KIM. I don't know, I don't care but unless they've got a good reason, they're not welcome back.

TUVA. Alva's right, we need a boat.

MALIN. Great, okay, but, seriously, why?

KLARA. BECAUSE SOME OF US MIGHT WANT TO LEAVE ONE DAY!

KIM. Klara.

MALIN. No, it's okay, it's fine, but let's remember that now, today, anywhere else in the world is a war zone. Strictly speaking, we don't need a boat. We only need food, water and power.

EBBA. We've got the power under control.

ELIN. And the water-traps are working like a dream.

MOA. Not that we're getting much help.

ALVA. What about the rest of the world, though? If the world's been reset by a war then, doesn't it need new ideas?

KIM. Shut up, Alva.

BASIC JANE. No, she's basically right, basically, this set-up, the leader, everything, it was supposed to be temporary. When did we decide that these roles were the ones we'd be stuck with –

MAJA *suddenly stands and everyone watches her in silence.*

MAJA. I can't listen to any more of this. Suggesting there are people better at what Elin and Moa do? At what Ali and Ebba do? At what I do? If you want us to start down the track of who's most efficient, I can tell you exactly how short you are on the amount you're supposed to have caught this week, do you want everyone to hear that?

BASIC JANE. I'm basically just –

MAJA. You're 'basically' derailing an important meeting with your own agenda. The missing boat, as Malin said, changes nothing about our daily life. We've worked hard. We've relied on one another. And you can all rely on me. But these questions, undermining confidence. 'Should we basically change roles?' 'Should we build a boat?' 'Should we build a boat to leave our safe, warm and comfortable home to go to a war zone and talk to people sick with radiation poisoning about our ideas?'

MAJA *laughs. A few people join her in laughing.*

Alva, love, there may be no bad answers but there are bad questions.

EBBA. That's true.

ELIN. Some questions just scare people.

MOA. They do.

EBBA. We should change The Code.

MALIN. Then we're agreed, we'll just carry on as before?

MAJA. No. We work harder. Grow more, cook more and catch more. Work makes this place.

MALIN *starts a smattering of unconfident support and then begins to usher everyone out.*

MALIN. Great, brilliant, now, you all know your roles, Maja will send me around with any changes but for now we're just going to keep working on making this place amazing, okay?

MAJA. Basic Jane. Hang on a sec.

MAJA *waits until only herself,* BASIC JANE, MALIN *and* KIM *are present.*

If The Code is written somewhere visible, then before continuing with BASIC JANE, MAJA *silently instructs* MALIN *to get on with rewriting it accordingly: 'There Are No Bad Answers But There Are Bad Questions.'*

Have you got something against the leader? Against The Community?

BASIC JANE. No, I'm basically –

MAJA. Because The Community is The Leader, The Leader is The Community. And you haven't contributed much except criticism, recently. Not much fish. Not much meat.

BASIC JANE. Basically… It's basically –

MAJA. I'm reducing your rations. We each have a role to play. Mine is to speak for everyone. Earn your food. Kim?

KIM *shows* BASIC JANE *out.*

Alone with MAJA, MALIN *has the courage to ask a question.*

MALIN. Maja, can I have a word?

MAJA *looks at* MALIN.

Okay, cool. Um. Just, everything you just said was brilliant, it was amazing but I do think some people are starting to get a bit... You know I'm a positive person but people are... worried. And no one came here for ever, that was never part of the plan, so maybe...

KIM *returns.*

Maybe, because we're, you know, survivors of this war, we should, perhaps, like, look for others. Other survivors I mean. I don't mean that we leave just that we put the periscope up a bit, look around, see if it's safe. That could be a part of the plan with a boat, I mean because, even if didn't use it, if we just tried building it, together, bit of teamwork, might, just –

MAJA. Malin, this all sounds a bit... Doesn't it, Kim? Doesn't it sound a bit – What's the word?

KIM. Weak.

MAJA. Yes, especially after I increased your responsibilities, it really does sound a bit weak.

MALIN. Okay, does it? Okay, I just meant that people might benefit from a project to all, you know, so.

MAJA. In spite of the war, you want The Community to just... end?

MALIN. Um, that's not quite –

MAJA. You did just talk about this not being for ever, didn't you?

MALIN. Well, I meant, to ask if maybe we all thought it might be safer now than –

MAJA. Sounds like a bad question to me.

MALIN. Yeah, no, I just –

MAJA. You don't think of yourself as above The Code, do you?

MALIN. No, I meant, a project, we could do with a project, just because there are tensions and –

MAJA. I left you in charge of helping people to get on, didn't I?

MALIN. Sure, and, well, maybe there's, with all that's going on, people might need something bigger, to believe in, I mean. We all left everything we knew behind to come here because we believed in something bigger and now... We just need something bigger.

MAJA. I'm going to give Kim your job, Malin. You can be her assistant.

MALIN. Okay. Okay. Right. Brilliant.

MAJA. Bye, Malin.

MALIN. Okay, cool. I'm just... So, I'll just um... Great.

MALIN *leaves*.

MAJA. Kim, pass me the face paint.

KIM *finds and brings the paint whilst* MAJA *readies herself*.

Let's give them something bigger to believe in.

KIM *watches whilst* MAJA *gradually begins to paint herself as the tribal leader of The Community*.

FOUR

Some months later.

FREYA *and* TUVA*'s tribal markings have almost faded away.*

FREYA. Trial? As in criminal, Tuva? As in a trial that people put criminals on for actual crimes? Tuva, are you saying there's gonna be an –

TUVA. Actual. Trial.

FREYA. But how's that – What's the – And what's it for? What's the crime, Tuva, what's she supposed to have – You know, actually, actually, criminally, done, what's she done?

TUVA. Broke The Code.

FREYA. Broken The Code!? Why would she break The Code? Everyone knows, you don't break The Code, war and that, you don't do it, Tuva, and, now there's gonna be some kind of – of –

TUVA. Trial.

FREYA. Trial to find out and work out and decide on and work out –

TUVA. Punishment.

FREYA. Punishment, exactly, Tuva, punishment for – for – I mean, she's – She's – So, punishment for –

TUVA. Henri.

FREYA. I mean, Henri, Henri's the cook, Tuva, she's our not very funny, funny cook, she's not, you know, is she? She's just not, so a trial seems a bit, a bit, doesn't it? It does, it seems a bit –

TUVA. It's happening now.

FREYA. Now? Right now, Tuva? The trial's happening now? And we're not – ? Shouldn't everyone – ? Isn't it sort of about everyone – ? Isn't that – ? What about Agnes? Does Agnes even know that her sister, that Henri, her sister's on – on – facing – Tuva, does Agnes know?

TUVA *takes a toke on her inhaler.*

Someone should tell Agnes, if Henri's gonna be, someone should probably –

TUVA (*exhaling*). Let's tell Agnes.

***

ALVA *is looking at something some distance from where she and* AGNES *now stand.*

AGNES. All animals kill each other. Sometimes for food. Like this. Sometimes not. It's natural. Vegetarians, vegans, not natural. Kindness is unnatural. Wars, bullying, they're natural.

A little pause whilst AGNES *decides whether or not to admit this:*

I stole a knife from the kitchen.

ALVA *looks at* AGNES.

I wouldn't do anything, I just really don't want anyone to steal any more of my food.

ALVA *looks back towards whatever she was looking at before.*

Haven't seen the shore in ages. Not even from the tower. Air seems thicker. Like something's gonna happen. Or has. Maybe it's thicker because of the war. Or maybe this thing's drifting further away. Do you think Basic Jane really tried to swim all that way?

ALVA *doesn't answer.*

Is that a bad question? Am I breaking The Code?

ALVA *doesn't answer.*

You've been here a long time now. Long enough that your
mark should have faded.

ALVA. I like what it – Repainting it, I mean. Reminds me that
some ideas, take work. Need sticking at, basically.

AGNES. When my sister said we were going away to change
the world, I was so excited. Travelling, disappearing, real
life! But now I think about it, I think, 'if we wanted to
change the world over there, why did we come here?'

ALVA. Quiet now, Agnes.

AGNES. But, Alva, no one talks about –

ALVA. You'll scare off basically all the animals, alright? Now,
shh.

After a brief pause, FREYA *and* TUVA *arrive, urgent and
concerned.*

FREYA. You need to come with us. Both of you. Both of you
really do really need to come with us. Now because it's
really, it's really, isn't it, Tuva? It's really –

TUVA. Your sister's on trial.

***

ELIN, MOA *and* EBBA *are holding* HENRI. KIM *is holding
her Taser.* MALIN *and* KLARA *watch.*

HENRI. It was a joke! It was a stupid joke.

KIM. You broke The Code!

HENRI. How? I don't even get how I broke it, how can a joke
break The Code?! Which rule? The one about working? The
one about questions and answers –

KIM. Yes!

HENRI. What? How?

KIM. Malin.

MALIN. Great, okay, thanks Kim. Because, Henri, that rule is actually about undermining people's confidence in The Community.

HENRI. They're jokes! I've got more, dim light bulbs or bright light bulbs, watt's the difference? Two 't's' in watt's. I was handed a leaflet to help me with my anger-management issues but I just LOST IT! Did you hear about the angry gymnast? She FLIPPED! Are they breaking The Code? Are they undermining?

EBBA. It'll be easier if you shut up.

HENRI. Other people have done worse! Signalling the shore during watch, fighting over rations –

KLARA. Kim, this isn't right.

KIM. The group decides what's wrong and right, Klara, not you.

AGNES *arrives, followed by* ALVA, FREYA *and* TUVA.

AGNES. What are you doing to my sister? What are you doing?

KIM. Can someone get rid of her?

ALI. Agnes, come here.

AGNES. Get off!!

ALI *grabs* AGNES – AGNES *screams,* HENRI *and* AGNES *struggle against their captors; all the members of The Community are present and disturbed, shouting and arguing before…*

MAJA, *painted like a tribal chief, arrives, slowly, and all the arguments and struggles fade to silence.*

When she is satisfied with the silence and ready to begin the trial, MAJA *nods to* KIM.

KIM. Henri's been undermining The Community with jokes about you.

HENRI. No, no Maja, all I said was – It's not even funny, I just said, 'How many free-thinking, independent political outcasts does it take to change a light bulb?' Right? And the punchline was just 'Don't know, ask The Leader.' That was it, not big, clever or funny. So...

KIM. Malin.

MALIN. Brilliant, thanks Kim, um, so, it's just that jokes like that one actually make it sound like you think we all just follow orders here, like this isn't actually an equal and – and – um...

KIM (*holding up the Taser*). Henri should be punished for the good of the herd.

AGNES. No! Leave her alone!

Everyone begins to shout and disagree whilst HENRI and AGNES panic.

Suddenly, MAJA holds up her hand and everyone instantly falls silent.

MAJA. Henri, you broke The Code upon which we all depend. Kim, punish her.

Everyone holding HENRI lets her go – holding her Taser, KIM edges towards HENRI.

MAJA begins to hum. Everyone gradually joins in making a rumbling and ominous sound.

HENRI scrambles to escape KIM's approach but no one is willing to stand between HENRI and KIM.

HENRI. Kim, don't. Don't. You said that's for cows, I'm a person, Kim, it's me. Don't.

TUVA steps between KIM and HENRI.

TUVA. I've got a question.

Humming, danger, everything suddenly stops.

FREYA. What are you doing, Tuva? Tuva, what are you – ?

TUVA. If there wasn't a war, and we had a boat, could we send Henri to shore instead?

KIM. There is a war.

TUVA. But, is there? Because, we've got no radio, no phones. One night, when I was on watch, I told Maja this, I saw lights on the shoreline, lights from towns and homes. Lights we said none of us had seen since we heard about the war. I saw them.

MAJA. That doesn't mean the war is over.

TUVA. And I saw a plane. I saw a plane with its lights on. A normal-looking plane. And boats. I've seen boats when I've been on watch. Fishing boats. Those normal big boats with boxes of stuff on them. Delivering stuff. If the world war was still happening, wouldn't that all have stopped?

MAJA. We spoke about this, Tuva. Everyone is supposed to report the watch directly to me.

TUVA. Yeah, but Eve and Evie were the only ones who actually saw evidence of a war, right? So if they knew that there really was a massive war, why did they leave? And if all everywhere is a war zone, why didn't they come back?

MAJA. Tuva, these are bad questions, you're upsetting people, you're breaking The Code.

TUVA. No, they're good questions cos if there's no war, we don't have to hurt Henri, we can –

A clicking sound, TUVA *silently collapses.* KIM *has Tasered her.*

A ripple of shock around the group as TUVA *wheezes on the ground.*

FREYA. She needs her inhaler. Someone give her her inhaler.

MAJA. Do it again.

KIM *Tasers* TUVA *again.*

Everyone screams, panics, people try to escape and the lights snap out…

***

...a small light illuminates MAJA*'s face in the dark. While she speaks, glowsticks, candles or torches are illuminated, we gradually begin to make out the faces of* FREYA, MOA, KLARA, ALVA *and* KIM. MAJA *is out of breath, frightened and making a concerted effort to look like she is unshaken by what has just happened.*

MAJA. Okay. There was a conflict. Mistakes were made in the past. People were under pressure. They broke The Code, but we won't let our instincts get the better of us. We will not be divided. We're better together. If we can get back to our core values –

ALVA. Agnes had a knife, Kim attacked people –

MAJA. That's what I'm saying, I'm saying that people let their instincts get the better –

ALVA. Everyone's gone, Maja. They were desperate, they tried to swim, because of you!

KIM. Shut up, Alva.

KLARA. Kim, did you really just –

KIM. You're not in charge, Klara.

MAJA. Kim, it's okay. There was a power cut, people panicked, but that was, four or five hours ago now and what's important is the future. If people decided to leave then that just makes this a new beginning, doesn't it? We're all in this together. Aren't we, Klara?

KLARA. What just happened?

MAJA. We hit a turning point is what happened. And if we're all going to get around it, we need to work through it together. Like a family. And every family needs someone who's good at speeches. You're good at speeches. When you arrived, I thought to myself, I thought 'She's good at speeches, must keep tabs on her.'

KLARA. Keep tabs? Were you keeping me away from Kim?

MAJA. Klara, please stop living in the past. We need a new direction. I propose we wipe out The Code, start again, maybe a change of name. What shall we call ourselves, Klara? Freya?

FREYA is either giggling or crying, it's hard to tell.

FREYA. That's... Hah, look, that's weird, isn't it? It's weird, this cos, this is her inhaler. Tuva's inhaler, look. No, it's just – It's actually quite funny, isn't it? It's, isn't it, Tuva? I mean...

ALVA. Kim, do you even know what you did?

KIM. I make sure people get on, Alva, it's what I do.

MAJA. Exactly. And that was impossible the moment that people started to behave like animals. Screaming, jumping into the sea, running away, hiding? We survived, which means that we're the future, what happens next is for us to decide. Isn't it, Klara?

KLARA. She's been using all of us.

MAJA. That is so lazy. It is so easy to criticise. Admit it, you've got no ideas of your own, have you? Now's your chance, prove me wrong, lead, go on. What do we do next?

KLARA. We leave.

MAJA. Wow. Great idea. With no boat, how do we leave? Where do we go? Lead the way.

KLARA. I think we should...

Everyone looks at KLARA.

We should...

Everyone waits but KLARA does not have any new ideas.

MAJA. As soon as the sun's up we'll divide into teams and clean the place up. We can start by clearing away the er... What shall we call it? Klara, we need to call this something that isn't going to traumatise everyone whenever we talk about it.

KLARA. Incident.

MAJA. Thank you. We'll clear away The Incident and then we can have a conversation about how we want to run the, um... new name, Klara?

KLARA. The Family.

MAJA. Yes, The Family. Once we've cleared up The Incident we can begin by writing a new –

ALI (*in the dark*). I can sort out the power.

MAJA. Great, okay. Who said that?

MOA (*illuminating* ALI). Ali's bleeding.

MAJA. We can fix that can't we, Klara? Alva, Moa, help her stand.

ALVA. Stop pretending everything's fine, it's gone wrong. All of it. Even if it started as a new idea it filled up with old ones.

KIM. Shut up, Alva!

ALVA. It's our fault, it must be, did we give up or something or stop trying?

KIM (*pretending to be calm*). Okay, Alva, come here a sec.

ALVA. WE HAVE TO BE BETTER THAN THIS!

The lights suddenly flick on to reveal HANNE *stood in the middle of the room. She is utterly composed and calm. Her cleanliness makes her seem utterly alien here. The floor is smeared with blood.*

HANNE. I don't know what you lot did to the power supply but it's a mess-sss-ss... It's broken.

FREYA. Hanne?

HANNE. Sss-sorry, my head's not what it was. Do I know you?

MAJA. What are you doing here, Hanne?

In the light, we can see that ALI *is the source of the blood.*

HANNE (*indicating* ALI). That one should probably get to a
   hoss-spital.

FREYA. Hanne, where have you – ? Have you – ? I mean…
   What?

KLARA. How did you get here, Hanne?

HANNE. Boat. Eve and Evie brought me my boat back. The
   one from here. They sss-ssaw I was back online, found me in
   the hoss-sspital. Told me you lot kicked Sss-sam out.
   Sss-said they'd bailed on the whole thing but not why.
   Thought I'd come and sss-see what was going on for
   myss-ss–

MAJA. Eve and Evie are traitors, Sam attacked you and they
   left.

HANNE (*clearly disbelieving* MAJA). Oh, yeah?

   HANNE *looks at* ALI.

   Best get that one on the boat. We'll take her to a doctor, call
   her family –

ALVA. What about the war?

HANNE. War? What war? There is no war.

MAJA. Hah! No war!? Alva, Moa, do not leave. As leader, I
   forbid it, for your own good.

   ALVA *and* MOA *help* ALI *up and out*.

   Come on, she's not thinking straight. Hanne's clearly got
   something wrong with her.

HANNE. I have, actually. Forgotten what the doctors call it,
   but… head damage. My memory's like, when you wake up
   from a dream and don't know what's real and what's not.

MAJA. See? Brain damage, she just said so. Of course there's a
   war.

HANNE. There's a radio in the boat. Put it on. There's no war.

MAJA. There is, Hanne, you're just –

HANNE. Funny this cos the lass-st thing I really remember, like, properly, is arguing with you.

FREYA *leaves*.

You reckon Sam attacked me then, yeah? Cos the doctor said that whatever hit the back of my head, must've been blunt. Like, a brick or um, an oar. I can't actually tas-ss-ste things now. Only textures. I actually, I ate a rotten apple the other day by accident.

MAJA. Klara, you're clever, you know that even if there isn't a war now, there will be soon and we need –

KLARA *leaves*.

Now, only MAJA, KIM *and* HANNE *are left*.

HANNE. Can I ask, did you hit me in my head?

No response.

Maja, it's pretty obvious you hit me in my –

No response.

MAJA. You wanted everyone to go. You wanted us to stop, to go home and tell people our ideas.

HANNE. I wanted to ssh– to ssh–

MAJA. To share!? Who would have listened? You would have ended *all this* to tell people who didn't want to hear, things that they didn't want to know. I protected these people. Kim, you understand, don't you? It's better to save those you can, make things better for a few than to fail at changing anything, isn't it? For people to succeed, others have to fail.

HANNE. But Sss-sam must have sss-suspected. After you hit me in my head, how did you make her leave?

KIM *drops the Taser.*

Didn't other people want to go home? Why didn't they all just go? Or… is that why that girl said that thing? Did everyone actually believe there was a war? Was that your idea?

MAJA. I did what was best for The Community.

KIM *leaves*.

HANNE. Eve and Evie had money. Was that from you? From all of our money, was that the kitty?

MAJA. Have you any idea what I sacrificed for this place?

HANNE. I think I do, aa-actually.

HANNE *picks up* KIM's *Taser. In fear,* MAJA *tries using all of her oratory skills to win* HANNE *to her side*.

MAJA. Put it this way, okay? A train is out of control, it's heading for five people who are stuck on the track. You can flip a switch, which sends the train down a different track with one person on it or you can do nothing. What do you do? You get involved. You flip the switch and save who you can, because it's the right thing to do. I protected who I could from the world out there, from you and your ridiculous ideas. You wanted us to go home, abandon the only place that's ever been any good, to change the whole world?! That's just not realistic. That's not saving anyone, they would have laughed at us and The Community would have been finished. You were a danger. Everything I've ever done was for the good of these people. I gave them freedom from responsibility, choice, ideas. I took care of them. I can't go back to just being... me. Please, Hanne. Please.

HANNE *leaves*.

MAJA *sits alone*.

FIVE

Almost a year later.

LISA *and* LUCY *are wearing uniforms; are they school uniforms or the uniforms of a correctional facility?*

LUCY. She'll be here. Just wait. Every day, she comes here and stares.

LISA. Stares? What at? The industrial estate? There's nothing there.

LUCY. Maybe she likes all the rust and that.

LISA. Weirdo.

LUCY. All the broken machines, maybe they're, I dunno.

LISA. Why would she come and stare at that stuff?

LUCY. I just said, I don't know why she does it, I just know she'll be here.

LISA. Do you think she killed anyone?

LUCY. No, I don't think she killed anyone.

LISA. Not all of them came back. Something must have happened.

LUCY. Are you scared?

LISA. No. A bit. I'm just saying that I don't think we should take her advice.

LUCY. There's no harm in asking what went wrong.

LISA. There is if she's mental.

LUCY. We can still find out what went wrong, can't we?

LISA. Not if she's not mental, that's what I'm saying.

LUCY. Well let's talk to her and find out.

LISA. Alright. But if she's mental, I'm leaving.

LUCY. Fine.

LISA. And you can't just talk at her. Not if you want her to answer questions.

LUCY. I'm not just gonna talk at her.

LISA. Let's just find out some stuff, then leave.

LUCY. I don't talk at people.

LISA. Shh... She's coming.

> ALVA *arrives in the same uniform as* LISA *and* LUCY, *no tribal markings, cleaner than ever before. She stands and stares at the audience. Maybe she can see us.* LUCY *and* LISA *build up a little courage before:*

LUCY. Hey. Hi. Um. It's nice, isn't it? Looking at the erm, those old structures out there.

LISA. Yeah, all those old crumbling machines and, the rubble and that.

LUCY. Nice.

LISA. Right. Nice.

LUCY. Yeah. Anyway, we've been talking and we just wanted to ask –

LISA. Say something about why, first.

LUCY. Yeah, so, um, really, we're just sick of this place. Of where everything's heading, of being totally unable to change anything anywhere and we were thinking, why not try something else? Why not take control, you know?

LISA. Lucy, questions.

LUCY. Yeah, so, we wanted to ask about the place you went to, The Community, we wanted to –

LISA. Say what, though.

LUCY. What?

LISA. What we want to know.

LUCY. I'm doing that.

LISA. Okay, do it then.

LUCY. We just wanted to say that we get it. We get why you went there. We get what it was for.

LISA. We do.

LUCY. And we want to know why it went wrong.

LISA. Because…

LUCY. Because we need to know because…

LISA. We have to change everything or the sea levels are gonna rise, the population's gonna keep growing, wars, refugees, pandemics and the world's gonna end. So…

ALVA. Basically, you want to go to a different place.

LISA. Yes.

LUCY. Yeah.

ALVA. So that you can change this place.

LUCY. Um.

LISA. Yeah.

ALVA. If you want to change things here. Stay here.

LISA. I knew it. She's mental.

LUCY. No, wait, what do you mean?

LISA. She probably wasn't even there, come on, let's go.

With whatever she has to hand (Tipp-Ex, mud…?) ALVA begins to paint the palm of her hand.

LUCY. We can't change things here, that's the whole point, no one listens to us or cares, the only way we're gonna change things is by going somewhere else, starting afresh. Clean slate.

ALVA. It won't be a clean slate because you'll be there. And you're not a clean slate.

LISA. Come on, Lucy, she's doing something weird, let's go.

LUCY. What do we do? This is why we want to leave, because we can't change things here –

LISA. Thank you for your time, enjoy staring at broken stuff like a crazy person.

LUCY. Lisa!

ALVA. I stare at all of those and I think, every single one was an attempt, failed or not, doesn't matter, at answering a question.

LISA. Lucy, we didn't want to talk to her about a load of broken old machines.

ALVA. What's the biggest question you can think of?

LISA. Let's go, she's not helping.

LUCY. What do you mean the biggest question?

LISA. Fine, I'm leaving, bye!

She does so.

LUCY. Biggest question, 'Why aren't there laws to make everyone in the world equal?' Or 'What would the world be like without money?' Or 'Why should we bother trying to heal sick people if the planet's overpopulated?' Or –

ALVA marks LUCY's face in the style of The Community.

ALVA. There are only good questions. You make things work. You are the community, the community is you. Stay here, change everything.

The End.

www.nickhernbooks.co.uk

facebook.com/nickhernbooks

twitter.com/nickhernbooks